Note from the Author

I believe in God's sovereignty and compassion. I am learning to let go of self and to hold onto someone that can do whatever he pleases. Sometimes life is cruel, sometimes it is full of suffering, physically and psychologically. A spiritual solution to meet difficult trials has become my goal. God's word carries with it no uncertainties. I want it to saturate my mind and heart.

The *Pastoral Health Care Series* was created through unexpected heart disease (open heart surgery), cancer (medication and surgery), a stroke and major head injury after a car accident that also resulted in the death of my wife. I am writing this because it is helping me to develop an adequate level to supernatural, psychological and physiological adjustments. It may help you as well. It has brought me security.

—John F. Gillette, D.Min

John Gillette's writings flow from a lifetime of experience. It is one thing to write out of a knowledge based on research. It is an entirely different thing to write out of a depth of life experience. John has both. As a pastor who has cared for the needs of a congregation, as a husband who has experienced the tragic loss of a wife, and as a child of God who has walked through the joys and pain of following the Lord, John has so much to offer in this series. From the opening pages, through to the very end, you will be blessed by the insights, loving tone and encouragement you receive from this series. God has used John greatly in ministry and will continue to use him through this life-giving series.

—*Josh Mateer, D. Min.*

True, illustrative, practical stories are like windows that unlock Bible truths and promises. Along with a masterfully orchestrated short stories should come the truth that God's Word and love has been experienced by His servants as they partner with Him in the work of rebuilding the Kingdom. A gifted teacher, Dr. Gillette lives an ordinary life abiding in Christ and being an obedient servant of the Lord. As he sees God working in his life, and in the lives of those to whom he ministers, his faith is refreshed and he is encouraged to press on through life's uncertainties.

Only a lifetime dedicated to nurturing, ministering, teaching, and keen insight through the power of the Holy Spirit, can produce such poignant stories that teach and challenge.

—*Mulonge M. Kalumbula, Ph.D.*

John's books give us hope and light. He reminds us that through Jesus we are never alone. I have certainly needed that reminder in my life and in my practice. In holding a patient's hand, and helping them through a condition or disease, reminding them that they are never alone has become the greatest gift of health care.

—*Linda M. Kunce, D.C.*

The series reminds me that Jesus knows what it's like to live in a human body. I have received Jesus and His forgiveness, but as the book suggests, I also have the power from the Holy Spirit. His books have encouraged me to gain courage through prayer and confidence in Jesus to meet my needs. John's honesty is very special to read as he reflects on his own life and struggles. I like his explanation that "the soul is where the emotions are and the mind is where the thinking takes place". It's been good for me to read that God works through weakness, and learn that John found God with him in the middle of the struggles.

—*Arvid W. Vandyke, Ed.D.*

Discovering God's Counsel is a book full of great spiritual truths from someone who has developed a very close and deep relationship with Jesus through his life. John provides a meaningful and inspirational testimony, with examples from his own experiences, of how relying on God's Word and promises can give you the power, hope, and peace you need to overcome life's struggles and challenges. The Scriptures he chose in his book were on point and helpful. It was an enjoyable and wonderful read.

—*Thoa Reyna, J.D.*

John has written a user-friendly and practical series for anyone desiring to live beyond the superficial and venture into the supernatural. The world needs this *Pastoral Health Care Series*. Pastors and followers of Jesus need the insights from John's lifetime experience of walking with God and caring for His people through the power of the Holy Spirit. John has brilliantly show that God is enough, God's love is real, God's counsel is enduring, and God reigns supremely. This important series will serve both the church and the world for many years to come.

—*Kizombo Kalumbula, Jr., Ph.D.*

Glorify
GOD

Other Books by John Gillette:

Discovering God's Sufficiency

Going Beyond Ourselves and Experiencing the Supernatural

Pastoral Health Care — Part One

Discovering God's Love

Confirming God's love through the evidence of historical facts

Pastoral Health Care — Part Two

Discovering God's Counsel

Applying his spiritual solution to meet difficult trials

Pastoral Health Care — Part Three

Discovering God's Kingdom

Finding a way to understand ourselves in a complex world

Pastoral Health Care — Part Four

Discovering God's Heart

Feeling God's heart pulse is our daily challenge

Pastoral Health Care — Part Five

"Christianity is the Impartation of a divine vitality"

Glorify
GOD

SO WHETHER YOU EAT OR DRINK OR WHATEVER
YOU DO, DO IT ALL FOR THE GLORY OF GOD.

1 CORINTHIANS 10:31

JOHN F. GILLETTE
Adult Instruction

ANNA HAMERSMA
Teen Perspective

Chapbook Press

Schuler Books

2660 28th Street SE

Grand Rapids MI 49512

www.schulerbooks.com/chapbook-press

Distribution contact:at jjgillette@comcast.net.

ISBN 13: 9781948237192

Library of Congress Control Number: 2019935310

Cover photo: Pexels.com

Cover Design: Frank Gutbrod Graphic Design

Printed in the United States of America

This book is lovingly dedicated
to my friends of the
Pastoral Health Care Ministry.

Table of Contents

CHAPTER 1

What is the foundation to glorify God?

Jesus said, "All that the Father giveth me shall come to me." This refers to God's sovereignty in my salvation (Romans 8:29, 30). He continues in saying "and him that cometh to me" (Ephesians 1:3-6). This is my responsibility to respond. Then he ends the invitation with a guarantee "I will in no wise cast out."

The process begins with belief. "Everyone who sees the Son and believes in him" (6:40). God works through faith and faith is provided as a gift (Romans 12:3; Ephesians 2:8, 9). Listen to what Jesus has to say — don't murmur or become hardened in the heart. Keep a clear perspective and mindset. My heart was opened through his Word which actually penetrated my mind, will and emotion.

Believing involves faith (II Peter 1:1). When I believed in Jesus (John 1:12), I received the gift of faith (Ephesians 2:8, 9). Faith is the ability to choose to fellowship with God, to obey him, to love him and to acknowledge him in all areas of life through complete submission and aggressive trust.

Through faith I have been forgiven (Acts 26:18). I have a living relationship with God (Romans 1:17). I have been justified (Romans 5:1). I have a life indwelt by God (Galatians 2:20).

Faith is personal and is based on the character of the one I believe (Romans 4:17-21). It is not based on emotion or circumstances. It accepts the promises of God as true and interprets them on the basis of the attributes of God. My personal salvation was a response to God and is based on who he is (Matthew 9:28, 29; John 1:2). It was easy for me to trust Jesus because he is God. The miracles and his claims have brought me into his family. He said, "I am the bread of life." Jesus is able to give life and sustain it. My hunger and thirst has been fully satisfied through him. My relationship with God includes trust, intimacy, obedience and love. Without Jesus, life is only an existence. I had to receive or reject his invitation.

Jesus said, "I am the light." As each year in my life slips by, I see more darkness and sin around me. In this world of depression, I have discovered that Jesus shines as the light. Jesus is the very light of God that has come among his creation. Jesus is the guide and the means to understanding life and direction.

He said, "I am the door." Jesus is the entrance into God's family. Through him I have access to a life that God wants me to have. On one hand, he offers safety and on the other security. I am thankful that I have gone through that door and have experienced new life and vitality

He said, "I am the Good Shepherd." Jesus gave his life for me on my behalf and for my benefit. He is a gracious shepherd who provides for everything I need. He is efficient, skillful and kind. He loves me and cares for me. He is aware of my necessities before I am.

His quality of care is beyond compare. He is indeed a good shepherd, "the Lord is my shepherd, I shall not want" (Psalm 23). He said, "I am the resurrection." Jesus not only takes care of my temporal earthly needs but more importantly, he provides eternal life. I think the bottom line to all he says and the basis for absolute truth is the resurrection. I have placed my trust on that truth. I have been set free and there is no more frustration or futile living.

He said, "I am the way." He says come and I will take you. You cannot miss the way because I am the way. He is not only giving advice, direction and counsel. He takes me by the hand and leads me personally (Psalm 27:11).

He said, "I am the truth." I have confidence because moral perfection finds its realization in him. He is the final key to life. He speaks with final authority in words adapted to human understanding (Psalm 86:11).

He said, "I am the life." The way is the means of reaching the Father. The trust defined the righteous standards of the way. The life originated with God and lifts me out of my sin to him. "In him was life and the life was the light of man" (1:4). Christianity is the impartation of a divine vitality. "I am indwelt by the Spirit of God" (Psalm 16:11).

He said, "I am the true vine." He is real and genuine. Jesus is the source of the heavenly life. He is the only solid foundation to build upon. It is a 'must' to abide in him. This means unbroken connection is maintained. It is a constant active relationship with Jesus. "By their fruits you shall know them" (Matthew 7:16). I believe in the death and resurrection of Jesus Christ for my sin and justification with God. God's counsel involves belief.

Teen Perspective

As teenagers our life is full of so many distractions that we often forget to take time out for Christ. Christ invites us to HIm, and we should accept it whole-heartedly. Believing can be hard, especially as we are caught by peer pressure every day. We need to ignore the calls to the evil things of this world and commit everything to Christ and invite Him into our hearts. Teenagers have their own kind of language that they use. Jesus is the bread of life. He gives life and he takes life. When someone we love is taken from us we often become mad at God and question why He would take someone so precious to us, but we need to realize that everything that happens is God's will. If it's not God's will, it won't happen. The teenage years are the most critical years of a person's life. It's when God paves the way for the rest of our lives. As we get older we realize all the bad things in the world around us. Jesus is the light of our world, and he lights up our world that is full of many dark things. Many teenagers go through a stage of depression, and Christ is the only solution to that. Another thing many teenagers go through, is a stage of insecurity and comparing ourselves to others. God will take us by the hand and lead us as the Way. We never need to doubt God. Sometimes teenagers doubt God, because they don't know enough about Him or their emotions lead them in a different direction. It's true, teenagers don't like talking about their faith. They want to make their own choices, but in the end they will realize that adults know more than they do. Christ is the Good Shepherd, and will supply all of our needs. He not only takes care of our physical needs, but our mental and spiritual needs as well. We need to rely on God to find our way in life.

CHAPTER 2

What is the resource to glorify God?

As I delight in his law (Scripture), I will be blessed. The promise "Blessed is the man who walketh not in the council of the ungodly . . . but his delight is in the law of the Lord" has laid the foundation (Psalm 1:1-2). I grew up believing in the Bible. I am extremely glad that I can say that. I do not take it for granted. I have had to unlearn a few things but the primary fundamental doctrines have been planted well into my brain waves. In those early days, if someone asked me to walk across the lake, I would have believe that God could accomplish it. If you asked why I believe, the answer would simply be that someone did it in the Scriptures. As long as they had their eyes on Jesus, no sinking took place. This belief remains secure because my spirit, soul and body have been entrusted in faith to Jesus Christ.

Everyone has to make a decision about the Bible "the sure word" (2 Peter 1:19). There is no escape. You may cherish, read, ignore, respect, dissect, study or hate it, but a decision has to be made. I began to read in the Bible and reflect on the fact that even though the original was written centuries ago, it is pertinent for me today. The Bible repeatedly speaks in terms that involve all generations. Jesus claimed, "Heaven and earth will pass away, but my words shall not pass away) (Matthew 24:35). The prophet Isaiah said, "The grass withers, the flowers fade, but the Word of our God stands forever" (Isaiah 40:8). It claims within itself to come from an all-knowing, all-powerful, personal God. You can laugh at the Bible and you can think that it is not relevant today. You can be a skeptic, religionist, agnostic, atheist, satanist or just a naïve person with good ethical standards, but the Bible is still for you.

As I was reading it, I couldn't help realize the uniqueness of it. It is different, it is one of a kind, it has no equal, it is a book written over a 1,500-year span and it was written over 40 generations. It was written by more than 40 authors from every walk of life including kings, peasants, philosophers, fishermen, poets, statesmen, scholars and more. It was written in three continents; Asia, Africa and Europe. It was written in three languages; Hebrew, Aramaic and Greek. It covers hundreds of topics. Yet the biblical authors spoke with harmony and continuity from Genesis to Revelation. There is one unfolding story; God's redemption of man.

There are many reasons why the Bible is important to apply to ones life. Its dependability is connected to its uniqueness, the canon, bibliographical test, internal evidence, prophesies fulfilled, historical geography, archeological evidences, miracles and its transforming power. Jesus Christ has made a direct challenge to my will to trust him. He says, "I have been standing at the door and I am constantly knocking. If anyone hears me calling him and opens the door, I will come in (Revelation 3:20). I discovered that when I accepted Jesus Christ as my Savior and believed he died on the cross for me and that he was resurrected, through faith my life has been changed from the inside out. I am convinced that the Bible is dependable because of the divine genius who has put it together. It has fulfilled the promise of blessing.

Holy men from God spoke as they were carried along by the Holy Spirit (2 Peter 1:21). The genius of this record is through the Holy Spirit moving upon, in and through human authors. The translation of God's thoughts and will to humanity is through language and inspiration carried along by the Holy Spirit. The Bible (66 books in the Old and New Testaments) has had a divine intervention. "No prophecy ever resulted from human design" (2 Peter 1:21). "We have a more sure word of prophecy" (2 Peter 1:19). We are not permitted to judge the Bible by our experiences but we must judge our experience by the Bible, 'the sure word.'

I am convinced that the Bible is dependable because of my spiritual understanding. "No prophetic Scripture can be explained by one's unaided mental powers" (2 Peter 1:20). The spiritual origin of the word necessitates spiritual understanding. Natural men cannot receive spiritual truth. The whole concept of scriptural ministry indicates that the minister of the New Testament is "not of the letter, but of the spirit, for the letter killeth but the spirit giveth life" (2 Corinthians 3:6). "It is the spirit that beareth witness because the Spirit is truth" (1 John 5:6). I cannot intellectualize or bargain with God, by faith I understand. The foundation and solid ground is the Holy Scriptures. Anyone can read the Bible but without the Holy Spirit's guided intelligence, the information is worth little. The study of the Word of God brings confidence.

I am convinced that the Bible is dependable because of my relationship with Jesus Christ. "These are written in order that you may believe that Jesus is the Christ, the anointed one, the Son of God and through believing in cleaving to trusting in and relying upon him, you may have life through his name" (John 20:31). The life is in him and not through any religious duties however beautifully performed. It is terrifying to know that this plain word, this testimony of Jesus, can be in a man's possession and he can miss the God of revelation. When we miss Jesus, we miss what God wants us to know. The great aim of the Christian life is not simply to know a set of ethics, but that "I may know him" (Philippians 3:10).

I think that everyone will come to a point in their life that they have to be convinced whether the Bible is true or not. My own mind and heart had to be convinced even though I was trained as a child and young adult. I appreciated my early foundation but I had to learn, decide and discover my own answers. I was in Chicago taking special studies at the American Conservatory of Music. One evening I picked up a book dealing with many reasons why I shouldn't believe in Christianity and the Bible. I had to come to terms with following the Bible all the way, partially or not at all. Satan tried to be deceptive in my mind and the council of the ungodly raised some questions. Amazing as it might sound, because I have delighted in the study of God' Word, the Bible, it began to convince me. Many scriptures came to my mind when my soul was troubled. Jesus said, "Let not your heart be troubled, ye believe in God, believe also in me...I am the way, the truth and the life" (John 14:1, 6). I threw the other book away. It really didn't have solid reasons in it. It just gave testimony of many Christians in the church that have been poor witnesses.

As I was walking on the shore of Lake Michigan and looking into the starlit sky above and the blue waters below, the Holy Spirit reminded me of the Bible verses that I had learned years ago. The witness of divinity and my own spirit were united and I was truly blessed. The council of the ungodly will lead you astray but his Word will bless your life. I believe in the dependability of the Scriptures. They continue to bless me in so many different ways. God's counsel is dependable.

Teen Perspective

If someone asked me to answer the question, what is the resource to glorify God in one word, the answer would be the Bible. Many teenagers think they can glorify God by staying away from bad things and going to church. That's not all there is to it. The Bible has laid the foundation and we need to build on that. Many people grow up without the Bible, which isn't good. The Bible will guide us through our life in good times and in bad. All it takes is a little true faith, and anything can be possible through Christ. Teens don't believe in this, because it's too big to grasp. Just a little faith and I could move a mountain, no way. As we get older we realize that it's true. It says it right in the Bible and everything in the Bible is completely true. We need to make our own personal decision about reading the Bible. We can reject it or we can make the right decision to read it and to apply it to our lives. Many teens think they don't need the Bible or

Christ. They can do everything without that, but they will soon realize that it's not true. We can't do anything without Christ's help. God's Word is forever. Everything will go away eventually, but Christ's Word will stand forever. We need to apply the Bible to our life. We can depend on it because it's Christ's Word. He never lies. Anyone can simply read the Bible, but it takes a true believer to apply and understand it. There's many things in the Bible that are hard to understand, especially for young people, but we can pray that God would reveal His word to us. We need to have a personal relationship with Christ. Everyone comes to a time in their life where they question whether the Bible is really true. The Bible has always been true, is true now, and will continue to be true. There's nothing to doubt about it. Reading the Bible shouldn't be a burden, it should be something we delight to do.

CHAPTER 3

What part does fellowship have in glorifying God?

I have been redeemed for something far beyond myself, my time, my space and my history. I am a citizen of another world. "I must view clearly this world, embrace the world beyond and live by the power of the resurrected world within."

The world I live in is the domain of my adversary. I will experience the effects of this place. Through my recent experiences, heaven has become more real and relevant. Heaven is not a spiritual fantasy land. It must be my transforming point of reference. The threat of death is simply the door to all that is better. The resurrection of Christ and his post-resurrection appearances have given a sense of the reality of the world to come. I am empowered and energized with this truth. I am a child of Christ's kingdom. This took place when I believed in him and committed my life to him. The king reigns in my life. I am learning that my life does not belong to me. I am not to manage it through my own passions, pride or personal prompting. This world does not offer safety, security or satisfaction. All things in life have to be seen in light of the kingdom to come. I have to be surrendered to the king that lives within me. I have to practice obedience to his Word.

Heaven is not a by-product for my faith. I do what I do in life for the eternal kingdom. If I lose sight of this or am not aware of it, I will miss the mark. I can conquer this fallen world and live with a guarantee that the kingdom of God will reign eternally and supremely with no rival and no threat (I Corinthians 15:2-28). This is possible through Jesus Christ's death, resurrection and ascension. I will be sustained through his grace "for thine is the kingdom, and the power and the glory" (Matthew 6:10). I have to become preoccupied with eternity and heaven.

Heaven is my all-consuming point of reference. I have to reflect on the eternal kingdom's values and live them out on this earth. My roots have to be based on eternity and not on earthly things (John 3:2). My home is heaven. Confidence and courage will drive me forward to conquer in this world because my faith is grounded in eternal values.

Fellowship is the key emphasis and is provided by a God who is true and whose promises are sure. Jesus Christ spent forty days here in his eternal bodily form and then disappeared into the world to come. Biblical hope is established on God's promises. It is easy to believe because I enter every day into fellowship with his indwelling presence. It is a growing process.

Fellowship produces security. It is sure. I have an inner assurance that perseveres with eager anticipation (Romans 8:24, 25). Things may get tough but I have trust that Jesus Christ has provided. I trust God to keep his Word. He has in the past and present and will continue in the future. I will be with him some day (John 14:3).

Fellowship provides fulfillment. It fills the emptiness and despair of the soul. It gives life meaning and direction. It provides for that inner drive to hold onto something secure. It brings excitement to life's adventures and satisfaction in the journey.

Fellowship develops my relationship with Jesus Christ. My life on earth is only a fleeting moment. Eternity is forever. I will sit at his feet as he unfolds the mysteries and miracles of both the macro and the micro elements of his marvelous, wise and intricate design.

Fellowship increases confidence. Sometimes death is fearful. I have to learn to embrace it because the fact is that dying is gain. I am encouraged as I die to self on this earth. This prepares me for heaven. I believe that heaven is real. As I affirm that truth in the depths of my soul. I will be free to live for Christ, even it if requires earth-side loss (Philippians 3:8, 9).

Fellowship is the key to hope. The resurrection of Christ proves that heaven is real. There is life after death. What can possibly distract me? I live for eternity. The more I make heaven my primary goal, the more I will be transformed. When I am for heaven, I will be contented, satisfied and fulfilled (Colossians 3:1, 2). I maximize my faith when I rely on my fellowship with him. No more struggles with my identity. Living for myself is not pre-eminent. I live for the kingdom to come and the kingdom that is within me. My behavior, attitudes, actions and responses relate to who reigns over me — Jesus Christ.

Teen Perspective

Why are teens afraid to admit that heaven exists? Why is anyone afraid to admit that heaven exists? Maybe it's because they don't want to believe it, or maybe it's because they want to believe it but they think it's too hard. Heaven is real, there's no way of going around that. We are too focused on the earthly things around us that we don't spend time thinking about our heavenly home. We need to reach past the easy things, and go for the things that are hard to grasp. Teenagers think that everything they need is right here on earth, but what they don't realize is that there are things that are much more valuable in heaven. What we do in life doesn't affect our life here on earth as much as it does our heavenly life.

We are living for the eternal kingdom. All this is possible through Christ's death and resurrection. Many people forget that nothing here would be possible if it weren't for Christ's sacrifice. Our physical roots are here on earth, but our spiritual roots are planted in heaven. Teens often question how they can have a relationship with God, if He's in heaven and we're here. We can't see Him, we can't have a conversation, so how can we have a relationship with Him. It's simple, through His word. Fellowship gives us meaning, security, confidence, and hope, all key things in glorifying God. We need to direct all things away from ourselves and aim them at the person who they should be on, Christ.

CHAPTER 4

How does relying upon God's promises provide glory?

I hear a lot of talking about health now. When I am with the older set of people, the conversation always refers to some part of the body that is not working well or hurts. When I am with the younger set, the conversation is about what gym they belong to. I like being around my students because the subject does not usually come up and when it does, it is with a positive attitude. The government is talking about health and insurance companies are discussing the cost of health. I would like to share what God says about health sickness and suffering. I have put my arms around Psalm 103:3 where it says "Bless the Lord . . . who heals all the diseases."

The Psalmist starts with "Bless the Lord, O my soul" and concludes with the same words. The delightful text consists of twenty-two verses, which is the exact number of letters in the Hebrew alphabet. It is a great hymn book of the church. When we are hurting, we must turn our attention to the God who has created us. All our senses and faculties should be placed on blessing the holy name of God. Our innermost self is inflamed when we are suffering and either we will magnify the Lord or reject him. I would rather recount all his benefits. He renews us like the eagles, he performs with his sovereign grace and he has removed our sins.

We have a corruptible body, a death-doomed body. There is the promise of the redemption of the body for which all true believers wait. When the Lord returns, we shall have that redemption changed into his own likeness and our bodies will then be like his glorious body. When we face health issues, let us remember healing is possible if it is in his will. If it is or not, he says,

"I am with you" (Psalm 23:4). This brings a sense of confidence. His presence is within us and he has no time or space limits. He encompasses everything and everywhere. "In him we live and move and exist" (Acts 17:28).

His eye keeps us in his sight. His guidance is available. We have to learn to let his instruction flow into our hearts and minds. His negatives are a part of his positive program. He leads even when we feel him or not and he keeps his promise, "I am with you and will keep you wherever you go . . . I will not leave you" (Hebrews 15:5). In sickness we can find assurance that he is near and nothing is out of his knowledge to know.

His victory is close at hand. He will provide a way of escape. This means that he will lead us, give us security, provide strength and enable us to find peace. Wherever we go, God goes. He is in us, around us, over us, under us and beside us (1 Corinthians 10:13). He knows our needs and will supply (Philippians 4:19). He will wipe the tears for he sees us (Genesis 16:6). The provisions that are needed are in his fingertips ready for action. We do not have to be anxious or fearful. He is the freedom giver. He surrounds us (Isaiah 41:10). He says, "I will help you, I will strengthen you I will uphold you."

"Your suffering is not in vain, it has a purpose" (1 Peter 2:19-21). Just at the moment of need, he is present on the scene. He provides protection and will carry us through. Sometimes it may seem that he is not near but as we focus or even when we cannot, he says "I will guard your heart and mind" (Philippians 4:6, 7). These are loving words that I have recited in my mind over and over again. They will keep us safe, strong and secure. I challenge you when in ill health or a bad circumstance to regain strength through claiming these promises. Stand back and watch God's hand at work. It really does work!

We do not suffer apart from the knowledge of God. Do not be intimated by all the talk. God knows all the details. Think about God's character rather than his creation. He is in control. Let the big picture rule your life, not the suffering. There is no promise of trouble-free living only power to endure the trouble that is inevitable.

"Have mercy upon me O Lord; for I am weak, O Lord, heal me" (Psalm 6:2). God is not against me when I suffer. He cares about me enough to save every one of my tears (Psalm 56:8). Through the tears, "he has heard my supplication the Lord will receive my prayer" (Psalm 6:9). I have confidence that when I have been willing to go to the secret place, the shadow of the Almighty, there will be comfort. Jesus Christ is the secret place of the Most High. Before suffering occurs, I have learned that thinking right is necessary. An ounce of prevention is good to practice. If we think correctly when we are well, the process will fall into action when we are not so well.

A conscious awareness of the Holy Spirit, our helper, is necessary. I have done this through reciting the Lord's Prayer (Matthew 6) and the shepherd Psalm (Psalm 23). As God takes up residence in me, I begin to live in his shadow and experience his hand covering me. Comfort is a result of continuous dwelling in him. His superiority, sovereignty and sufficiency abound and will produce a wave of strength over my suffering. When I cannot see or understand something, God can. My feeling of apprehension, concern, worry, dread and anxiety will come under the shadow of the Almighty. When I recite God's words and dialogue with him I am strengthened. His will will be done and "I shall not want" will bring security. I have learned that God is all powerful all wise, all loving and never changing. I am in his hands. He reminds me that I cannot do it but he can.

Reflecting on the past has produced the reassurance that God has my best interest in mind. I have had to commit the sickness to the Lord through being more aware of him than the illness. I have had to release it to him because he is quite capable of handling it. His word has been implanted in my mind and heart. A daily breathing in of the Holy Spirit is absolutely necessary.

God's presence was at my birth. Three babies that were unexpected were born at home in a small upstairs apartment during a cold winter storm. Some premature issues followed but God's hand was present. It was an amazing God-touched miracle. God's presence was unique in my childhood. I was running to school and took a short cut. I came head on with a car as I turned the corner. The driver did not see me and I did not see the car coming. I tried to get out of the way but the gravel under my feet made me fall. The front wheels of the car came to a screeching halt right next to my lower back. Did an angel stop those wheels from rolling over me?

God's presence was seen in my teens. During an act of kindness, my hands were infected. The doctors tried medicine, radiation and acid. I could feel the acid eat away the infection. The Holy Trinity provided aid. My one hand was held by Jesus and the other by the Holy Spirit. The heavenly Father gave me a sense of his presence.

God's presence was experience in my adulthood. I was standing by the pulpit of my church. I would imagine the people in their favorite seats as I rehearsed my Sunday sermon. Suddenly I had a lot of pain and dropped my

Bible and fell to the floor. I had experienced a silent heart attack. The doctor determined what to do. I witnessed God's intervention.

Relying on God's promises brings abundant living even in suffering. "My hope is in Jesus. Hear my prayer, O Lord, listen to my cry for help" (Psalm 39:7, 12). There is no one whose understanding of life has come close to his. He will help us. I am learning that when I think correctly, it will involve reciting God's Word. This leads to reflecting on personal experiences. Reciting and reflecting will climax in reliance. Reliance on God's promises will bring rest, courage, strength and expected hope.

Teen Perspective

As teenagers, we often ask the question why. Why would God let my loved one get sick? Why would God take my loved one away from me? Why is this happening to me? God never promised us an easy life, He promised that He would help us get through it. There is going to be pain and sickness and death, but God says He is the God who heals all our diseases. God doesn't just heal the physical needs, but the spiritual ones as well. God watches over us and is always with us, which means there is no need for us to fear. It's important that we put our trust in Him instead of in ourselves. We need to commit our lives to Christ and live fully for Him.

CHAPTER 5

Why should I glorify God?

In my time of 'trouble' (surgery), I responded to this verse "and call upon me in the day of trouble" (Psalm 50:15). I definitely called on God for help. The verse continued with "I will deliver thee" (hospitalization). God promises to work everything out for my good and his glory certainly became a reality in my life. It ended with "thou shall glorify me" (recovery). I have wanted to glorify him from day one. How this would turn out would be in his hands. I had to let go of myself. He is in charge.

The glory of God refers to his worth (Genesis 31:1), to his power (Genesis 45:13), to his excellence (1 Chronicles 16:10,24,27,35), to his greatness (Deuteronomy 5:24), to his holiness (Isaiah 6:1-3), to his divine manifestation (Hebrews 1:1-3, and to his loving grace (John 1:14). When I personally think of his glory, I think of these words; splendor, superiority, sovereignty, Savior and shepherd. His glory is the total of his essence and attributes. God is glorious because he is God.

I prayed "help me to glorify you through this experience in my life." I had no idea how it would bring honor, praise and glory to himself. It started with my primary focus. He is my refuge (during surgery), strength (during each initial day) and present help (during recovery). This was established through my belief in the Son of God. My salvation in Jesus Christ was secure.

My spiritual transformation is based upon a personal relationship that continues to grow. Negative thoughts will not be found in my mind. I believe in a positive redemption. My counsel will come from the law of God. The Bible has become a dependable source for me. Its claims come from an all-knowing, all-powerful, personal and only existing God. I am convinced through careful research, study experience and inner witness.

The foundation for my coping with the unexpected open heart surgery and cancer is based upon God's promises. I have had to learn to listen to his words and then do them. "Drawing near to him" (James 4:8) has brought a sound, beneficial, righteous, fruitful and pleasant result. As I draw near to him, he will draw near to me. The result will be his presence, love, grace, sovereignty, glory, justice and wisdom. I learned to handle the impossible through watching God work it out for his glory. He provides everything I need at the time I need it, not before or after, but at the moment. Before I entered into this journey, I had the right attitude toward God and life. I believe in God's goodness and I interpret life from his viewpoint.

My days will have gladness and sadness. I experience strength and weakness. I will succeed through victory and defeat. "The Lord is my shepherd, I shall not want" (Psalm 23:1). I have experienced some setbacks. The road is not always upward. It would be nice to say that the journey was pleasant without some doubt.

Human nature would not be natural if that was the story. Circumstances, anxious thoughts, stress and unexpected issues all contribute to the throwing of doubt into the path. I have to do something about this. My weary mind can be changed. God provides the refueling process. I am going to pursue glorifying God and understanding its meaning. Whatever happens, I will obey 1 Corinthians 10:31).

Teen Perspective

The most important thing in our life is that we glory God and trust in Him, the rest we leave up to Him. We can do nothing by our own strength. We glorify God in times of need and in times of happiness. We need to have a personal relationship with Christ and be rooted in Him. God does things for His glory, and He always provides. Whatever happens, God's got it.

CHAPTER 6

What part does salvation have in glorifying God?

L ife becomes a celebration as I follow Jesus. It involves his supernatural power. This power is received through the development of God's thoughts saturating my thoughts (I Corinthians 2:11,12). The more I think upon God's Word, the more I will think like God. His view of things will become my views. His attitudes will become mine. Knowing God's will causes me to pray in his will. It is exciting to explore the vastness of an infinite God. It is also exciting to see how I am wonderfully made (Psalm 139:14). Through my situation, I am more conscious of how the heart and brain work. I also refer this to knowledge and experience. The situation and the knowledge of God must be transferred to the heart. The brain and heart oversee complex systems that are necessary for life, the nervous system and the circulatory system. Each is encased in a protective fortress of calcium, one inside the cranium and the other within the rib cage. They are on the job all the time with no days off until death or the resurrection day. The human brain is the single most complex apparatus of all God's vast creative genius. It is the center of my nervous sytem and contains billions of neurons, each having thousands of synoptic connections. The heart is smaller than my brain but no less impressive. In an average lifetime, the heart contracts and relaxes two and a half billion times without stopping to rest. At 72 beats a minute, that is over 4,000 beats an hour and over 100,000 beats every day. In every heart, blood is drawn into my heart, filtered, processed and pumped back out again to every millimeter of my body. The brain is the center of my thinking and the heart represents my affection, emotion and personality. I have to learn to love the Lord with all my heart (Mark 12:30) and to keep my heart with all diligence for out of it springs the issues of life (Proverbs 4:23). Sometimes it is hard to get the message from head to heart.

The knowledge of God has to filter down into the heart. It takes nourishment from God's Word through observation, interpretation and application. I have to inform my thinking through contemplation. I will then understand his perspectives. I am all set as I respond to the text, "What think ye of Christ" (Matthew 22:42). I am learning to be a doer of the Word (James 1:22). This is absolutely necessary for me. My heart stopped pumping blood as a matter of fact during surgery. A life machine kept it pumping. After four bypasses and some valve work, it started to work on its own again. The nervous system, the circulatory system, the rib cage and the emotions and personality have all been affected. I discovered that the supernatural power of God can be infused in me through the Holy Spirit. The saturating of God's word through accepting its authority, the applying it and studying it will make me think like God.

Read from my devotional book "Thoughts to Ponder," pgs 7-8. The Bible says, "And he reasoned in the synagogue and persuaded the Jews and Greeks, and he continued teaching the Word of God among them" (Acts 18:4,11). I know of no other way to give the authority of the Scriptures than to continue teaching the word. I would like to reason and persuade you that the Scriptures ares a living, vital agency with supernatural power in itself. Read the promise, "For as the rain cometh down and the snow from heaven, and returneth not thither, but watereth the earth, and maketh it bring forth and bud, that it may give seed to the sower and bread to the eater; so shall my word be that goeth forth out of my mouth. It shall not return unto me void, but it shall accomplish that which I please, and it shall prosper in the thing whereto I sent it" (Isaiah 55:10,11). To the same purpose Jeremiah has written: "Is not my word like as a fire? saith the Lord; and like a hammer that breaketh the rock in pieces?" (Jeremiah 23:29). God uses his word,

"For the word of God is quick and powerful and sharper than any two-edged sword, piercing even to the dividing asunder of soul and spirit, and of the joints and marrow, and is a discerner of the thoughts and intents of the heart" (Hebrews 4:12).

The Bible is an ancient book for modern times. It is one book, one history and one story; one mind produced it. God himself became a man so that we might know what to think when we think of God. I could give all the evidences for scriptural authority but why don't you read the Bible for yourself and let it prove itself?

The Bible says, "As newborn babes, desire the sincere milk of the word, that ye may grow thereby" (I Peter 2:2). God has given his word so that believers may grow thereby. We haven't fulfilled our obligations to the word until application has taken place. The Bible is not only the source book for information but has life changing power for today. Growth in the spiritual life comes not merely from hearing but from hearing and doing. The Bible says, "the effectual doer shall be blessed in what he does" (James 1:25). "If you know these things, you are blessed if ye do them" (John 12:17).

The Bible has been given so that man's basic nature can be changed. "All scripture is given by God and is profitable for teaching, for reproof, for correction, for training in righteousness, that the man of God may be adequate, equipped for every good work" (2 Timothy 3:16,17). It teaches, rebukes, restores, trains for righteous living. It equips us to do the work that God wants us to do. The Bible convicts, regenerates, nurtures, cleanses, counsels, guides, prevents sin, revives, strengthens, gives wisdom, delivers and helps. The Bible alone realistically and sufficiently meets man's deepest problems, longings, needs and inadequacies. It provides the answers to man's needs for deliverance from the penalty of sin, for spiritual progress for victory, for guidance and for personal relationships and conduct. As we learn the Scriptures, let us apply it to our daily activities.

The Bible says, "Blessed are the undefiled in the way, who walk in the law of the Lord" (Psalm 119:1). What is wrong with reading the Bible? Why do people think it so strange? Some people have the idea that the Bible is just for the mentally weak, some people think it is for the ignorant, some people imagine that it is just for the shut-ins and some think it is only for the children. Why do the teens and young adults turn from it? I believe they do not go on to read it or believe it or study it or follow it. If we are going to walk in the law of the Lord, we must follow this pattern.

We need to study it through, that is, master a verse every day. Think of it and at the end of the year, you will have 365 verses in your heart and in your mind to bring about happiness, direction, peace and contentment. We need to pray about it. We must let each verse become a part of our very being, praying the verse into reality and then seeing the promises of God, as we claim them, change our lives. We must write down our thoughts. We cannot remember everything but our computer mind has it and we need to refresh our memory. That, of course, brings us to working it out. Let the Bible get in your heart and then live it out every day. It is not good only to study it through or pray about it or put it down or work it out, but we must also pass it on. We must talk about it. Let the word of God inspire and bless your heart. This takes discipline.

You cannot be lazy. Walk in the law of the Lord and you will find purpose and peace. As I learn to follow Jesus, life will become a celebration because it involves his supernatural power.

Teen Perspective

If we really search the Scriptures we can learn to better understand God's views, attitude, and thinking. God created our bodies with so many different parts that have so many different functions. He created us to love and glorify Him. The Word of God is the most powerful book ever written, which God gave us so we can grow in Him. It answers life's big questions. So then, why doesn't everyone read it? Why do teenagers and young adults turn away from it? Why do they reject the truth? It doesn't make sense. Maybe it's because they are afraid. Afraid because they know they are sinners in need of a God. That would be even more reason to read it! The Bible can truly change a person's life. It brings a meaning and a purpose to life.

CHAPTER 7

How can I live for the glory of God?

I can live for the glory of God through daily affirming the Scriptures where it says, "I will praise thee, O Lord my God, with all my heart, and I will glorify thy name for evermore" (Psalm 86:12). I am looking for ways to glorify God in my life. I want to live out the faith, love and hope I have experienced. My story has revealed how God used faith (the foundation of my life), love (the motivation behind my life) and the hope (that includes the others together with expectation in my life). The Bible says, "Let your light so shine before men that they may see your good works and glorify your Father which is in heaven" (Matthew 5:16). This refers to actions in my life. Do I display honesty, mercy, righteousness, kindness, gratitude, joy and patience?

The Bible says, "Herein is my Father glorified, that you bear much fruit, so shall you be my disciples" (John 15:8). Bearing fruit is a manifestation of my life in Jesus Christ. I can bear fruit through good works (Matthew 5:16), through purity (1 Corinthians 6:19, 20), through trust (Romans 4:19, 20), through unity (Romans 15:5, 6), through service (1 Peter 4:10, 11), through prayer (John 14:13), through subjection (2 Corinthians 9:12, 13), and through honesty (1 Peter 2:12). My personal response is found in 1 Corinthians 10:31, Whether therefore you eat or drink or whatsoever you do, do all to the glory of God." As I allow the word of Christ to saturate my life, I will glorify God.

Teen Perspective

Our whole life should be for God's glory. We should live for His glory. It can be seen through our actions. Do we daily practice the fruits of the Spirit? We should reflect on these things and ask ourselves those tough questions. 1 Corinthians 10:31 says it all "So whether you eat or drink or whatever you do, do it all for the glory of God." It doesn't say do most things to God's glory, but every single thing we do!

CHAPTER 8

What part does surrender have on glorifying God?

I have been able to follow God's plan of action in my life through practicing his promises. This scripture, Psalm 100:3, has proven to be profitable. Read the examples given to bring comfort. Affirm his intervention that provides peace. Accept his indwelling and experience victory. Adjust to God's illumination with hope.

Learning to live every moment in God's presence requires claiming his promises. In my book "Discovering God's Favor," I have shared God's faithfulness through using Psalm 23 as a foundation for my childhood events that needed a touch from a faithful God. Take time to read it because it will enhance your spiritual growth. I have great benefits in having a relationship with God the Father through his son, Jesus Christ and the guidance of the Holy Spirit. The divine genius is working daily on my behalf.

I am interested in accepting God's provision for unknown issues that come up in my life. I want to share how this Psalm-poem (Psalm 23) has secured the path for me. It starts with authority that can transform the seeking heart. Deity is suddenly facing me. I can handle anything with God alongside of me. All his attributes go into action. In my book, I write about his attributes and later I share thoughts about his name. They have become confidence builders. There is no losing of ground when I know in whom I believe. I have a growing intimate relationship. "The Lord is my Shepherd." It is hard to comprehend or believe but I have communication with God my creator-sustainer-redeemer and Lord.

There is no deficiency in my life. He provides the promise, "I shall not be in want." Contentment can settle me. Only he can provide such rest and peace. He is in charge and the controller of all things. The unknown is directed by his hand of mercy. This is only the beginning. I am able to shout and jump with joy because an infinite, holy, self-existent God in whom I have found has provided the way.

The flies and parasites that torment sheep can be found in fear, tension, worry, uncertainty and the unknown for humans. Panic, discontent, agitation and restlessness do not have to conquer me. I am going to put his provisions into action. The Scripture says, "Be still and know that I am God." (Psalm 46:10). I have to learn to be quiet. Quietness for some is a way of life. It can be a time to reflect, a time to create, a time to recover, a time to grieve, a time to rejoice or a time to listen to God. I have to put aside the barriers, schedules, outside interruptions and intrusions. Spiritual intimacy is a must. I think activities and the busyness of life have caused me to get off the right track at times. I have to close my eyes and lay down in the green pastures. As I lay down, I reflect in the fact that God the Father chose me in Christ before the foundations of the world (Ephesians 1:4). He predestined me to be adopted as his own (v5). I reflect on the fact that God the Son carried out God's plan of redemption by shedding his blood on the cross. He redeemed me through his blood and provided forgiveness for my sins (v7). I reflect on the fact that God the Spirit will enable me to respond in faith to God's love and has guaranteed my inheritance (v 13,14). This reflecting brings peace and security. This will help bring freedom from the unknown.

God says, "wait on me – I will renew your strength, don't run and be weary, don't faint but walk in the Spirit" (Isaiah 40:31). I know that God will be with me. He is alive and present whether I feel his presence or not. He will not abandon me. He says "wait on me." I have to rely on him and look to him for my source of strength. Psalm 23 provides what I need to succeed. I do not have to carry the burden of the unknown. God says, give me your burdens, tell me about them, give me your worries and concerns. When I do, I am like the eagle (Isaiah 40:31). As he floats effortlessly in the wind, I can do the same because the unknown is placed into God's hands.

I am able to experience rest as I reflect upon the God in whom I believe. I must affirm daily that:

- I believe in one and only one God and that he is a personal and perfect Spirit who is infinite.
- I believe his attributes describe him and that he is sovereign.
- I believe he will provide rest in the green pasture because he cares.
- I believe in one God who is a trinity and is co-equal, God the Father, God the Son and God the Holy Spirit, and all three are present with me.
- I believe that God has a plan for all creation and is carrying out that plan. He will provide strength for my part.
- I believe there are no surprises with God. He is carrying out his will through providence.
- I believe that Jesus, begotten by the Holy Spirit, is truly God and man.

- I believe that Jesus voluntarily accepted his Father's will and came to earth in humanity, lived a perfect life as the sacrificial lamb to take upon himself my sin.
- I believe that Jesus' atonement is the way to my acceptance by God and also the defeat of Satan.
- I believe that Jesus' death totally accomplished the ransom for my sin.
- I believe in Jesus' literal physical resurrection. His resurrection guarantees mine. Believing in Jesus assures God's rest for me.
- I believe that the Holy Spirit is involved in all the acts of God.
- I believe that the Holy Spirit was sent to comfort me and give me rest.
- I belicve the Holy Spirit is responsible for my regeneration and transformation.
- I believe the Holy Spirit indwells me and illuminates the Scripture to me.
- I believe that through the Holy Spirit I am able to affirm these facts that will provide rest for my spirit, soul and body.

As I learn to be in a resting mode, my mind and heart will hold onto the truth of God's Word. My thirst is quenched through his Word. As I allow it to saturate my mind, my soul becomes relaxed with his presence. His thoughts take control of my spirit. It starts with my spirit, then enters my soul and finally takes charge of my body. I have to learn to disallow the pollution of evil to enter my mind as I drink. The Scriptures will become my measuring rod to test everything. My quiet time becomes a restful, reflective and refueling experience. As I drink of the cool waters, it gives refreshing nourishment. I am putting his provisions into action. I can handle unknown issues in my life because God is equipping me through the Holy Spirit.

I am obtaining rest through recognition that God is giving the rest and a sense of well-being. As I affirm who he is and that he is in me, he produces the rest. I will follow him beside the quiet waters. I am not going to drink the dirty water that surrounds or creeps into the back door of my mind, but the pure water that flows from his Word. My thirst will be quenched because the Holy Spirit is doing the leading. I live in a confused and sick society. Christ comes quietly and invites me to come to him. He knows my heart, personality and soul. He has the capacity to satisfy. Only the Spirit and life of Christ himself will make me complete.

As my body needs water to stay alive, it also needs the indwelling of the Holy Spirit (I Corinthians 6:19) to quench my thirst. I cannot see him but his personality and presence are facts. His personality is proved in John 16:13,14. The pronoun "He" is used eight times to refer to the Holy Spirit. He is a real person because he comes, guides, hears, speaks, glorifies, receives and he shows.

It is hard to handle the unknown but with a counselor and helper like the Holy Spirit, I am able to succeed. To succeed, I have to follow his leadership by the quiet waters. When my heart is touched by him I have to respond. When his words make an impression in my mind, I must act. I have to practice repentance with honesty. I have to practice trust with loyalty. I have to practice obedience with love.

In my late teens, I wrote a little booklet entitled "A Touch of Heaven on Earth." I believe now, many years later, in the same things I wrote. If I want God's touch, I have to do what he wants. I have to learn daily to be sensitive to the Holy Spirit's presence. I have to stop resisting the Spirit. I have to stop saying no to his guidance. I have to stop refusing to yield to the Word of God as he brings it home to me. I have to be in a constant attitude of yieldedness rather than rebellion. I have to learn to stop sinning against the Spirit. I grieve the Holy Spirit when I break fellowship with him. Unconfessed sin has to be dealt with on a daily basis. I am not dealing with a force or power or influence, but with a person. The Bible says, "As ye have therefore received Christ Jesus the Lord, so walk ye in him." (Colossians 2:6). I received him by faith and the only way victory is obtained is in my dependence upon the Holy Spirit. He dwells in me and my heart has to be emptied of me and filled with him. The question is, Am I dominated by the Holy Spirit or by myself? Having a "touch of heaven" is through meeting certain conditions: stop resisting the Spirit, stop sinning against the Spirit, stop walking in the flesh.

Right at the time I think all is well, it seems everything will fall apart. The enemy knows my weaknesses. He certainly does not want me to bring glory to the Lord Jesus Christ. I cannot let my guard down. I have to realize that a battle is going on. At all times, I have to stand ready with offensive and defensive weapons.

I can face defeat. I can feel cast down. I can be distressed. I may be frustrated and experienced helplessness. I can even enter into depression. The struggles can be big in my eyes but not in God's eyes. I have to keep focused on him and when I take my eyes off of him, I will sink. Let's keep in mind that Jesus is a caring shepherd. In my spiritual dilemma, he doesn't become disgusted or fed up. I have experienced his love, compassion and tender care. He is ready to give reassurances, patience and restoration. In the path of life, there are many dangers. Restoration takes place when I am free of myself. God knows what he is doing with me. He is in charge. I am glad that he is ready to restore my soul.

I am glad God is ready to restore even when I have missed the mark. Sometimes I have forgotten that a battle is going on. As a musician-trumpeter, I have played "Sound the Battle Cry!" many times. Verse three says, "O Thou God of all, hear us when we call, help us one and all by thy grace; when the battle's done and the victory won, may we wear the crown before thy face." It seems suddenly in the midst of a calm, ordered and peaceful life, all the forces of Satan can break loose. He restores me through giving me understanding of the threefold attack. The act of creation is described as follows: "And the Lord God formed man of the dust of the ground and breathed into his nostrils the breath of life; and man became a living soul" (Genesis 2:7). The Scripture reveals that the body was made of the dust of the ground, that the spirit came from the breath of God and that the combination produced the soul (Hebrews 4:12). Satan's mind works against the spirit, soul and body of men. Against the body, he brings the temptations of the flesh. Against the soul, he brings the temptation of the world. Against the spirit, he comes himself or through one of his lesser agents.

I am not a casualty in the warfare. I can learn the subtle devices of the enemy, the devil. Let me begin with the flesh or body. I am not referring to the soft substance of the living body which covers the bones and is penetrated with blood. The body has a proper use of its every function and is normal, natural and moral. There is no sin involved or anything in connection with the human body itself. There is a human side apart from divine influence and it is prone to sin and oppose God. The body cannot run the affairs of the spirit and soul. It has to be controlled by the spirit and soul. When my will chooses to allow my body to dictate what it is going to do, then something is wrong. I am to abstain from anything that is in contrast to the principles of God's Word. I have to be so familiar with his Word that I will know what is right or wrong for me to do. It is not a bunch of rules but applied principles. Run from the enemy. The crucifixion of self has to take place. The enemy attacks the soul with the influence of the world. My senses are the focus. Whatever is drawing me away from the will of God is wrong to follow. If it keeps me away from Jesus, something is wrong. I cannot conform to the world's ideas. Conforming to the image of God's Son will show me what it means to not conform to the world.

Faith is the key word to build upon (I John 5:4), a definite turning away from the world "set eternity in the heart" (Ecclesiastes 3:11). Faith is a daily decision to respond to his Word in the correct way. The devil's greatest interest is my spirit. His desire is to keep me from God's guidance. The sins of the body and conformity to the world are terrible in themselves but the denial of God in the heart is unpardonable. Submission to God is absolutely necessary. Resisting comes next and putting on the armor of God will bring deliverance. In leaning on my own understanding (spirit-sin), I will fail to trust in the Lord with my whole heart (soul-sin) and will allow weakness in the body to flourish (flesh-sin). I am on the winning side with restoration bringing victory in the battle.

Like the sheep, I have to keep moving. I learned a long time ago (Isaiah 53:6) "All we like sheep have gone astray, we have turned everyone to his own way and the Lord hath laid on him the sin of us all." I like to go my own way but God knows what is the best way to go. Jesus said, "I am the way, the truth and the life" (John 14:6). Another favorite verse is found in Matthew 6:33, "Seek ye first the kingdom of God and his righteousness and all these things will be added unto you." I am like the sheep – blind, habitual and stupid. The little trails I follow become gullies. Turning to "my own way" simply means what I want. I have to learn to follow Jesus. He says, "If any man will follow me, let him deny himself daily and take up his cross and follow me" (Mark 8:34). I may at times give a mental assent to the idea but my will doesn't want to follow. This is the pivot point. The decision has to be made. "I will follow" means a rugged life of self-denial and attitude change. I have to deliberately put myself out on behalf of others. I have to be single-minded. I may have to stand alone. I have to learn to take a back seat. Self-determination has to change to dependence. Circumstances of life don't determine my attitude. Gratitude, peace and joy are seen in every situation.

Learning to cooperate with the Holy Spirit is the major focus. Right thinking will take place when my spirit and soul are in line with God's will. Learning to move on with his plan is necessary. He makes this possible by his own gracious Spirit who is given to those who obey (Acts 5:32). For it is he who works in us both to will and to do of his good pleasure (Philippians 2:13).

I think living righteously will produce correct thinking. My decisions have to be made with eternity in mind and his holiness. In verse three it says "path of righteousness" which is a pleasant and peaceful one because it is through God's name that provides his pure grace for the journey. I think following my own righteousness is worthless. It is built upon a self-achieved list of do's and don'ts. Righteous living and right-thinking involves:

- A relationship with God through belief in his Son.
- A realization that death with Christ and being raised with Christ brings newness of life.
- A recognition that God is doing the work on my behalf.
- A responsibility to get clean.
- A required cooperation with the Holy Spirit.
- A replacement of self-will for God's will.
- A removal of disobedience to daily obedience.
- A reminder to practice gratitude, peace and joy in every situation.

I have to adjust to God's thinking. Playing Christianity doesn't work. His path is full of responsibility and rewards.

There are many valleys I have crept through. I have learned to put the previous provisions into action. Now I can turn to the most intimate part of the Psalm — "the shadow of death." The sheep face dangers of rampaging rivers, avalanches, rock slides, poisonous plants and predators. I am fortunate to walk in the shadow of the Almighty. Jesus Christ has conquered death. I don't have to be air-lifted out of the situation. In every situation, in every dark trial, in every disappointment, in every distressing dilemma, I walk with the King. Every mountain has its valleys. The walk may be slow but it can be steady with Jesus. Intimate contact with Christ is the key. He says that he is with me. I have to learn to have an attitude of quiet acceptance of every adversity. Through the adversity, I can move to higher ground. My heart is full of thanksgiving when I realize God has given me a rod and staff to comfort me. The rod or club protects me. The rod becomes the extension of my arm. It is a symbol of strength, power and authority in any serious situation. The rod speaks of the Word of God. It implies the authority of Divinity. The staff provides care. The staff is a symbol of concern and compassion. It is an instrument of patience and kindness. The shepherd leans on it. It is a symbol of the Holy Spirit. The Holy Spirit will guide me, teach me, give understanding, give gentle promptings and counsel me. My reinforcement is provided through the Holy Spirit's constant presence and the use of Scripture against the enemy.

This power comes through his guidance, instruction, understanding, and gentle prompting. It is possible when I become intimate with Jesus Christ. Life can be complicated and cluttered. The Scripture calls for simplicity (Ecclesiastes 7:29). Cultivating intimacy with the Almighty will involve a changed life routine. In reading my spiritual autobiography, I discovered the necessity to stop. The triple career was exciting but too much. The decision was to simplify. Absolute silence has to follow the simplicity (Psalm 46:10). I have to make time for God. The picture is stillness, quietness, listening and waiting before him. This takes discipline but is indispensable if I hope to add depth to my spiritual life and be reinforced. There is no quick fix in becoming intimate with God. In my solitude, God does the examining (Psalm 139:1-4; 23-24). I have to do the confessing (I John 1:9). When I get rid of the complications of life, I am able to find a time for silence. In my silence, I am able to listen to God and make the adjustments. This will provide serenity in the soul. All these activities will bring me to complete trust (Proverbs 3:5,6). No longer am I preoccupied with working on the details in my life. Unqualified reliance in the living Lord takes place.

My life will have days of gladness and sadness. It will experience delightful days and dark days. I still have a great, sovereign, gracious and good shepherd who provides for me even in the midst of my enemies. He anoints my head with oil. He cares for the sheep and he cares for me. The overflowing presence of the Holy Spirit is continually overshadowing me. Coping with unknown issues turns into contentment when my conscious thought-life becomes anointed by the Holy Spirit. I can be free from the world's contamination through faith and acceptance. Just as I have asked Christ to come into my life initially, I need to invite the Holy Spirit to come into my mind to monitor my thought life.

God provides all the preparations to help me. He knows ahead of time my needs. I am blessed with the understanding that he is in charge (sovereignty). I am blessed with experiencing his goodness (grace). I am blessed with his love (mercy). I am blessed with his sufficiency (abundance). I am blessed with his resources (filling). These give me reassurance of his greatness, graciousness and goodness directed toward me.

As I learn to rely on God, his goodness and mercy will pursue me and I will always be at home with him. "I will never leave you nor forsake you" (Hebrews 15:5). I have a privileged position. No matter what comes, my treatment will be with goodness, mercy and his presence. I may have limited knowledge, understanding, wisdom and comprehension but I have an inner witness of the Holy Spirit. He provides confidence as I work through the provision of rest, refreshment, restoration, right-thinking, reinforcement, reassurance and reliance. No disaster, difficulty or dilemma will take charge of my spirit, soul and body. My serenity has its basis on a total reliance on God's ability to do the right thing and the best thing in any given situation for me. God's presence involves his promises.

Teen Perspective

God has made many promises to us, which for some people are hard to believe. We need to practice and claim His promises. We can trust God with our whole lives, because He's got it under control. He will provide for all of our needs. Surrendering our lives means giving everything to Him. We need to daily ask ourselves what we believe. Are we able to give our lives to Christ? If so, how can we do that? It won't always be easy, but God will give us rest. There will be times when it feels as if everything is going downhill, but all we need is faith as small as a mustard seed (Matthew 17:20) and give the rest to God. He can and will win the victory. The devil will be after us, and we will fall astray as lost sheep, but we need to look to our Good Shepherd. God is the way, the truth, and the life (John 14:6).

CHAPTER 9

What are some hindrances in living for the glory of God?

I will miss the mark in glorifying God if I fail to understand the greatness of God (Isaiah 40:25, 28). The very nature of God needs to be understood. He is infinite, absolute, unchangeable and perfect in all his ways. All I have to do is ponder on these attributes: his faithfulness (my doubt), his holiness (my sinfulness), his love (my selfishness), his sovereignty (my anxiousness), his truth (my falsehood), his absolute knowledge (my questioning), his powerful nature (my fear), his presence everywhere (my panic) and his lordship (my disobedience).

He is absolutely in control over all of his creation. He rules over the affairs of men and does whatever he chooses (Job 23:13). He can do whatever he wants to do simply because he owns everything (Psalm 24:1). All the details of my life will not escape him and whatever purpose he has for me, he will achieve. I will miss the mark in glorifying God if I fail to understand the goodness of God (Exodus 34:6). I have to learn to evaluate the person and work of God from God's perspective, not from my emotion and circumstances.

His goodness is found in his creation. If I understand that I was formed by and for him my life would become revolutionary. I was made to glorify him. I have been created by God, that determines my worth. I have been redeemed by God. That determines my peace. I have been created by God for himself. That determines my fulfillment. No longer is there confusion, failure, weakness and instability. His goodness has taken over.

God's goodness can be defined through reading Psalm 119:68, "Thou art good and doest good." He is good by his nature and by what he does. Every good thing bestowed and every perfect gift is from above, coming down from the Father of lights. God only produces that which is good. Keep in mind that God is sovereign. He allows things for reasons we do not always understand. There is no sin or defect in him. My challenge is to respond and rely upon his words, "No good thing does he withhold from those who walk uprightly" (Psalm 84:11). God can change negatives into positives. He causes all things to work together. When I reflect on God's goodness, my prayer is "Oh give thanks to the Lord for he is good; for his lovingkindness is everlasting" (Psalm 107:1, 2).

I will miss the mark in glorifying God if I fail to understand the graciousness of God. I will never forget a little chorus I sang as a child. It has three main emphases. The chorus became my theme song. It was based upon the New Testament book of Ephesians. "His very own, wonderful grace to his word is made know, chosen by the Father, purchased by the Son, sealed by the Spirit, I'm his very own" (Sidney E. Cox). God's grace is not deserved. It cannot be earned and be abused. Grace is God's unmerited favor. I would like to begin each day with "grace be to you" and end with "to the praise of the glory of his grace" (1:2, 6). Grace is the divine and free favor of God. It comes with tranquility and is a result of the reconciliation that has taken place between God and man based on faith in the union with the Lord Jesus Christ. The source of spiritual blessings comes from a heavenly Father and Jesus Christ. The blessings are unmerited. They are a product of the Holy Spirit. I am able to be blessed because I am 'in Christ.' This is the key. Nothing is too good or too great for God to bestow upon me. Grace goes before me because God has chosen. Jesus is my mediator (1 Timothy 2:5). Grace finds its foundation in the will of God. God's choice was eternal and his plan is timeless. I either receive or reject God's provision in Christ. Grace goes before me and enables me (Romans 8:29). Holiness is the positive side of a Christ like life (Hebrews 12:14). God expects me to live by his standards. Grace goes before me and provides for my adoption. I have been placed into his family. I am "his very own according to the good pleasure of his will" (v.5). The purpose of God's grace is to receive glory. He receives glory as I praise him in my vital relationship with his Son. God is totally self-sufficient. I cannot demand anything nor do I deserve anything. Living in his grace is my joy (Galatians 2:20).

Teen Perspective

Living for God's glory can be difficult sometimes. We have to do our part, and God has to do His. There are so many different words that we could use to describe God's greatness that the list could be miles long. But why is that important? To be able to glorify God, we first need to understand Him. His goodness can be found everywhere. We must receive God's grace instead of rejecting it. I have my duty to seek out God, instead of just waiting for Him to come to me.

CHAPTER 10

What part does support have to do with glorifying God?

My prayer is "cause me to hear thy loving-kindness...for in thee do I trust, cause me to know the way wherein I should walk; for I lift up my soul unto thee, deliver me" (Psalm 143:7-9). I have asked God to do it. I cannot do it on my own. I have a willing heart but am weak. My hope is fixed in the promises of God. He is faithful and he will bring deliverance. The fullest meaning of his faithfulness is found in the cross and the finished work of the Son of God. The reception of Jesus is the beginning of life (John 1:12; 14:6).

As I have traveled in this new life, I have experienced many trials. I am going to share some insight from the Old Testament (Psalm

40:1-17) and the New Testament (1 Corinthians 10:13) to compare what they have to say. It has helped me be assured of victory. In the New Testament it says, "There hath no temptation taken you." The words here can mean a trial which takes many forms like hatred, hunger, sleeplessness, pain, misunderstanding, worry and discouragement. It can mean testing which can help me grow in grace. It can also mean a temptation which is what Satan uses to weaken me. How I handle temptation is dependent on what I think and how I act and react. In Psalm 40:2, it says "he brought me up also out of a horrible pit." Sometimes I have experienced a deep sense of agony. It seems the trial has brought me to the bottom. Through Christ's humility and my substitute on the cross, he has delivered me from the pit through his death and resurrection. The overwhelming infirmities are no match to the mighty grace of God. The word 'many' in verse 5 reveals his marvelous works (Ephesian 2:7). In humility I have started on the path to victory.

Back to 1 Corinthians 10:13 where it says, "no temptation has seized you but such is common to man," I am reminded that I am not alone in this pain. My situation is not unique. God's promise is to help me in any situation. In Psalm 40:2, God refers to the 'miry clay' which reminds me of a thousand ways that I can be tempted and tested. I have found myself at times in a big mess but I am not alone because God is faithful. God knows all about me. He is fully aware of my problems. In this verse, God says he will not permit me to be tempted above that I am able. I am confident that I will not be tested beyond my capacity to endure. If I keep this truth in mind, my attitude and behavior will follow the right course. I have waited patiently for the Lord. "Blessed is the man who makes the Lord his trust" (v 1,4). Patience and waiting united will produce faith.

Faith is a decision to rely upon God's promises. God will provide during the trial a way to safety. In Psalm 40:1, it says that "God inclined unto me." This word contains the idea of bowing down. It is a fitting picture of the grace of God. The sinner is in the pit and crying out and God bows down to meet the need. The Lord bowed all the way down until he met me at the bottom of the pit. Now, through his resurrection, I bow down to him and receive victory. In 1 Corinthians 10:13, it says 'ye may be able to bear it." I can overcome my struggles by having my mind focused on the truth. He will set my feet on a solid rock and will establish my goings. He will give a new song and will reveal my testing to others. He will participate with me in victory. Now, pray the prayer, "cause me to hear…deliver me" (Psalm 143:7,8). Read Psalm 40:1-17 slowly and recite 1 Corinthians 10:13 between each verse. I have discovered in humility assurance of victory through this process. "Blessed is the man who maketh the Lord his trust" (Psalm 40:4).

Teen Perspective

We all want that one person in life that we can look to in times of need. God is the best person for that. God has never and will never let us down. In fact, He will do the total opposite. He will raise us up to do greater things. Without God, there really is no meaning or point to life. Yes, there will be times when everything feels lost and hopeless. Go to God, He can and will help you. Pour out your heart to Him, He will listen to you and hold you tight in HIs loving arms. Why do people reject Him then? He is that friend, He is THE Friend.

CHAPTER 11

What priorities should I pursue to glorify God?

I have to shine brightly to reveal good works to glorify God (Matthew 5:13-16). Because I am in Christ and he is in me, I can live out his beatitudes that will glorify him through my attitude and actions. I can discern my true condition before God. It is the spiritual awareness of the distance between infinity and finiteness. It is the repentant cry of my heart as I stand in the shadow of Calvary and look up into the loving face of the one who suffered in my place. It is serving in humility with meekness, hunger, mercy and righteousness.

I have to pray with boldness to glorify God. "And whatsoever you shall ask in my name, that will I do that the Father may be glorified in the Son" (John 14:13). Jesus wants to be involved with my daily life of prayer. To pray in his name means that I am praying in his will. I am learning to saturate my mind with his. It takes discipline, devotion and dedication. What a privilege it is to talk to God through his Son and the guidance of the Holy Spirit. Daily breathing should become a part of my breathing in his word and intimate communication with him.

I have to understand my identification with Christ to glorify God (Romans 6:4). I have died in Christ and I have been raised in his resurrection. This simply means that I may not allow any sin in my life and I must be characterized by all forms of virtue. Living in harmony with my union in Christ must be demonstrated.

I have to mix his word with faith to glorify God (Hebrews 4:1-3). I have to be more than willing to do God's will. I have to do it. I have to aggressively mix the Word of God with faith. I have to practice trusting God. This involves knowledge and application of his word, "Be ye doers of the word and not hearers only" (James 1:22-24). I must learn the word, put it into practice by faith and do it all for the glory of God.

I have to please the Lord with thanksgiving to glorify him. Thanksgiving should be spontaneous. It should be a daily activity in my life (John 6:11; 11:41). I am thankful to God for himself and for his greatness, goodness and graciousness. As I seek to understand his infinity, his attributes, his work and grace, I come before him in gratitude. Without his mercy, I would be lost. I am thankful for his counsel and how it endures generation after generation.

Teen Perspective

I should not be ashamed to say I am a believer. As a matter of fact, it should be a joy to tell people that. Glorifying God takes bold prayer. Does prayer simply become a habit, or do we really take time to think about what we're praying? We should pray in Jesus' name and for His will, not our own. When God lets His will be known to us, we must do it. It takes knowledge and trust, but if we have a true relationship with Christ, it shouldn't be difficult. Thanksgiving is one of the most important parts of daily life. God has given us more than we can even ask or imagine.

CHAPTER 12

What part does satisfaction bring to glorify God?

To change feelings, we must change thinking. Inaction will bring misery.[1] Learn to apply the Scripture to your life. The result will bring strength, support and steadfastness.

Learning to live every moment in God's presence requires applying his instruction. Out of all the promises I have learned, this one seems to cover all of them. As I draw near to him, he gives me the instruction I need to follow. He equips me to face whatever is before me. This provides the enablement and mindset needed to live a full and complete life (John 10:10). As he draws near to me, I am able to sense his

---

1   Christian Counseling, Gary R. Collins, p. 93

presence. This provides confidence and joy in knowing that he has my best interest in mind even if I don't understand at the time.

I am going to share what I am practicing in order to overcome weakness, temptations, health issues, decision making and just plain troublesome issues. Someone said, "thinking right always precedes acting right." I would add spiritual insight and application will cause us to think right and act right. I have discovered that the promises work. Put into action Jesus' words and you will find contentment and rest.

"Draw near to me and I will draw near to you" is found in James 4:8. James, the brother of Jesus, was used through the Holy Spirit to pen these words. James was ministering in Jerusalem. The church was persecuted and driven out of the city and scattered. He says do not be alarmed or sad. The child of God may rejoice victoriously even in the darkest hour. To rejoice I have to not only obtain knowledge (the facts) but it involves experiential knowledge (doing). Most of all, it involves an illumined heart (Holy Spirit counsel). I am excited to know that when I do not get it (the answer for difficult issues), I can always ask for wisdom (1:5). I can find the purpose in the predicament. I am not going to doubt God. He has given me faith and I trust the faith giver. God is all he claims to be.

I have to learn to listen to his Word and then do it. I have to learn to be submissive and live life with spiritual discernment. I have to learn to practice self-control. God's grace is at work. Practicing submission to God and resisting the enemy will pave the way for me to draw near to God and assure me of him drawing near to me.

Drawing near to God involves an attitude of helplessness which will result in enablement. In Jesus' own words, he says "Blessed are the poor in spirit for theirs is the Kingdom of heaven." (Matthew 5:3). He also says in his model prayer "Hallowed be thy name"(Matthew 6:9). He gives the instruction on how to draw near and he gives the source of power behind it. I have to come to the realization that dependence upon God is necessary. I have to acknowledge sin in my life. I have to receive and believe in Jesus Christ (Acts 16:31; Romans 10:9-10). His enablement takes place when a relationship develops with him and I learn what "thy will be done on earth as it is in heaven" means on a daily basis. I have become a member of the Kingdom of heaven. I have a double citizenship on earth and heaven. My life is nothing less than "Christ in you, the hope of glory" (Colossians 1:27). Natural life has a beginning but no end. My eternal life will provide fellowship with God for all eternity. My life on earth is preparation for heaven and drawing closer to him.

Helplessness refers to not being able to help oneself. To be "poor in spirit" means that I have emptied myself of me — now there is room to be filled. The world promotes self-sufficiency or at the present time (2010) government sufficiency, yet God dwells with the man whose heart is broken (Isaiah 57:15). When this decision is made, the promise of inheriting the Kingdom will provide enablement. Power, energy and strength are found in the centerpiece of God's attributes "Hallowed be thy name" (Matthew 6:9). This opens up a whole dimension of reverence, respect, awe, appreciation, honor, glory, adoration and worship. To hallow God's name means to hold his matchless being in reverence so that we will believe what he says and will obey him. When I live by faith and bear fruit in my character, I will exalt God's name. God has asked me to live in harmony with who he is and has stated this in his Word. I must understand my helplessness and promised enablement. When I fear God, I will have the necessary ingredient of life which opens the door to everything good (Psalm 111:10; Proverbs 1:7,8,13).

I know through personal experience God's enablement through helplessness. I can talk about sickness (heart disease, cancer) and about several friends with a variety of physical or mental illnesses. I can share about financial stress and looking for a job without success. I can include inferiority complex and the lack of confidence — the list is long.

Enablement comes through understanding the Biblical phrase "It is he that hath made us and we are his" (Psalm 100:3). I have seen this positive phrase bring spiritual enablement for many besides myself. We can be assured in our total dependence upon him that it will provide authority because he is all-powerful. I cannot Lord, but you can. Abiding in Jesus is the secret of enablement.

Drawing near to God involves an attitude of repentance which will result in comfort. In Jesus' own words he says, "Blessed are they that mourn for they shall be comforted" (Matthew 5:4). He also says in his model prayer "Thy kingdom come," heavenly comfort will come to us (Matthew 6:10). He gives the instruction on how to draw near, and he gives the source of power behind it.

I have come to the realization that repentance is necessary if I am going to draw near to him. I have asked myself often, "do I ever mourn for sin that has been allowed in my life; do I experience anguish over lost souls, and the disobedience of followers of Jesus?" I know that I can experience God's compassion through my repentance and be renewed.

Mourning refers to a sincere sorrow for sin. God hates sin. I should also. It grieves him but I like to make excuses for it. Tolerance, deception and blindness — add your own favorite word to the list that creates a blockage to growth. Repentance means a change of mind. It is a thorough change in the heart from sin to God. It is a gift of God (Acts 5:31; 11:18; Romans 2:4). I have to be mournful not only because of the consequences of sin and the baseness of sin but also the divine compassion provided in salvation.

Repentance will challenge me to put the Scripture into action…" put to death — whatever belongs to your earthly nature…" (Colossians 3:5). Sometimes I forget my responsibility. I have to make a personal decision to pursue holiness. I have to learn to put to death the misdeeds of my body. I have to destroy the strength and vitality of sin as it tries to reign in my body. Just think of it — my body is the temple of the Holy Spirit. He will do it. He is sufficient for this work. Conviction will start the path toward a holy life. Keep in mind "without holiness no one will see the Lord" (Hebrews 12:14). I want to be drawn near to God.

The world's values that are everywhere present must be replaced with God's. I have to let God remake me and not allow the world to squeeze me in (Romans 12:2). I have learned that only through God's Word can my mind be renewed. It takes conviction and obedience to pave the way to fulfill God's desires for me (John 14:21). The Scripture must be strongly fixed in my mind and heart. It will become the dominant influence on my thoughts, attitudes and actions. I like memorizing Scripture because I know it works (Psalm 119:11). I believe conviction and obedience linked together with confession will bring comfort in my repentance. Confession is necessary every day.

God hates sin and I must be sensitive to it. I must confess it and accept God's comfort in my repentance. I must let his Word work in my life. I must hide his Word in my heart. I have used the word "must" several times. It is important to do what I am trying to emphasize or I will fail. To understand what is right or wrong to do, I have to ask myself, "is it helpful physically, spiritually and mentally? Does it bring me under its power? Does it hurt others? Does it glorify God?" (I Corinthians 6:12; 8:13; 10:31).

Drawing near to God involves an attitude of surrender which will result in a controlled life. In Jesus' own words he said, "Blessed are the meek for they shall inherit the earth" (Matthew 5). He also said in his model prayer "Thy will be done on earth as it is in heaven" this meekness is characterized in heaven (Matthew 6:10). He gives the instruction and how to draw near, and he gives the source of power behind it. I have come to the realization that meekness in my life will bring about a controlled life. Meekness refers to living for the glory of God. There is no room for self-will. It is not thinking of asserting my own rights. Meekness is not weakness but a display of strength. Meekness is brought into my life through God's grace. I have to learn to accept God's dealings with me without resistance or dispute. No more rebelling or fighting against God. It flows from the heart of humility and submission.

I believe that when I have the three 'thys" in the right perspective in my life (found in Jesus' model prayer), I will experience the meekness characteristic. I am glad that the Holy Spirit makes this possible (Romans 8:26,27). I have to practice faith and the certainty of the Holy Spirit's indwelling. I have to surrender my will to his will. I have to place Jesus' name on everything. The word 'thy' emphasizes God's rule. His sovereignty is in charge. He has absolute control over all of creation. I have to live life in relationship with his sovereignty. I don't have to figure out the plan.

The sovereign kingdom rule has to be followed. Meekness and control are the fruit of obedience. I have to learn to switch on the confidence button by turning to God and away from sin, switch on the confidence button by allowing my inner judge of moral issues to be in tune with Jesus Christ, switch on the confidence button by making decisions through a righteous common sense and switch on the confidence button by obeying the special assignments given to me. "The Kingdom of God is not meat and drink but righteousness, peace and joy in the Holy Ghost" (Romans 14:17).

Drawing near to God involves an attitude of craving which will result in satisfaction. In Jesus' own words he says, "Blessed are they that hunger and thirst after righteousness for they shall be filled" (5:4). He also says in his model prayer "Give us this day our daily bread" (Matthew 6:10). He gives the instruction on how to draw near and he gives the source of power behind it. I have to come to the realization that craving after righteousness is absolutely necessary. Only when this takes place will I find contentment.

When I have a craving for something, I cannot leave it alone. It has a driving force behind it. It pushes me forward. This can be a good thing that takes place yet also bad. I am looking at the positive side and not the negative. Proof of my spiritual rebirth is found in my desire to pursue after righteousness with hunger and thirst. The inner passion is a blessing. Being poor/helpless, being mournful/repentant and being meek/surrendered will cause a deep earnest desire to search the Scriptures. This will bring satisfaction, fulfillment and contentment. Practicing having an appetite for good food is a good thing. What I eat will reveal the man I really am.

Craving after righteousness will take place as I study his Word. A few weeks ago I was looking at some of my previous sermons. They are bound into a dozen or so books. I found one based upon Psalm 119:33-40 — "quicken thou me — quicken me in thy righteousness." The word 'quicken' means in Hebrew to make alive, to refresh and in English it refers to a thought of adventure and becoming active. I discovered through activating the thoughts in verses 33-40 that they will produce a craving heart for righteousness. "Teach me" (v.33) indicates that a foundation has been laid. The master teacher has brought the lesson to my ears and has established my way. The teaching has made me alive. "Give me understanding" (v. 34) has brought discernment and correct insight. It is not only information and knowledge but a diligence to pursue it. Understanding has made me alive. "I shall observe" (v. 34); careful watching and exercising great care has made me alive. "I delight in the path" (v. 35), receiving the instruction, understanding the Word and careful observation has brought pleasure. A deep affection has been cultivated and has made me alive. "Incline my heart" (v. 36); through God's testimonies, my being has been made alive. With the right purpose in mind, the attitude is to covet Jesus Christ. "Turn away" (v. 37) allows my eyes to feast upon Jesus and not my own vanity. Help me to move in the right direction and be made alive. "Establish thy Word" (v. 38); my heart has been made alive through the respect and reverence that has integrated into my soul for Jesus.

"Turn away my reproach" (v. 39); I have learned that your Word is sound, beneficial, righteous, fruitful and pleasant. I have been made alive because your judgments are good. "Behold, I have longed after thy precepts" (v. 40); Craving for righteousness will be produced through an intense, sensitive and energetic response to God's Word. I have to realize the source of quickening is through the infusion of the Holy Spirit. I have to realize that I have to respond to his quickening. I have to make a decision to feed upon the Scripture. I am not a victim of worldliness or my own weaknesses. "Quicken thou me in thy way." This is possible because of Jesus' model prayer. He said "Give us this day our daily bread" (Matthew 6"11). This refers to all of my physical needs. When I am dependent upon him, he provides all my needs. Boldness in the Holy Spirit and confidence will empower me. I am thankful for the fact that he provides food, clothes, shelter and especially his presence in health or sickness. I have discovered this in his Word that has power to quicken me.

Drawing near to God involves an attitude of empathy which will result in mercy. In Jesus' own words he says, "Blessed are the merciful for they shall obtain mercy" (Matthew 5:7). He also says in his model prayer "Forgive us our debts as we forgive our debtors" (Matthew 6:12). He gives the instruction on how to draw near and he gives the source of power behind it. I have come to the realization that experiencing empathy will bring mercy.

Mercy is defined as being compassionate. Compassion is having a feeling of deep sympathy. Sympathy is the ability to share the feelings of another. This leads to empathy. Empathy is identifying with an experience of the feeling and thoughts of another. Someone told me that it is like getting in the skin of another. Mercy becomes a part of my life because I have obtained mercy. The Holy Spirit produces mercy. Jesus himself became the ultimate example of this when he cried from the cross, "Father, forgive them for they know not what they do" (Luke 23:34).

When I get in touch with God, I can feel his mercy at work on my behalf. It started when I trusted in him (Ephesians 2:4-7) and he gave me a clean heart (Acts 15:9) and peace within (Romans 5:1). When I receive mercy, I then can share his mercy with others. I pray that I can be sensitive to others that cross my path. I hope I can sense their hopelessness and need. I desire to come alongside of them.

Drawing near to God involves an attitude of authenticity which will result in seeing God. In Jesus' own words he says "Blessed are the pure in heart for they shall see God" (Matthew 5:8). He also says in his model prayer "And lead us not into temptation but deliver us" (Matthew 6:13). He gives the instruction and he gives the source of power behind it. I have come to the realization that purity will cause my heart to see God.

God is doing a work in me. He is conforming me into the image of Christ (Romans 8:29) whose image consists in "righteousness and true holiness." (Ephesians 4:24). Purity of heart is a part of my election and redemption (Ephesians 1:4; Titus 2:14). This is not sinlessness (I John 1:8) but the truth within (Psalm 51:6). It means a single heart. I am not divided between God and the world. I realize that this calls for radical living. The world praises pride not humility. The world endorses sin. The world is at war with God. Righteousness will cause persecution. Conflict will take place. Since my life has been transformed by the grace of God, I will see him. Daily faith will bring me into his presence. I might be called peculiar (Titus 2:14) but I have been chosen by the Father, purchased by the Son and sealed by the Spirit. I will see God.

Drawing near to God involves an attitude of harmony which will result in being called children of God. In Jesus' own words he said, "Blessed are the peacemakers for they will be called children of God" (Matthew 5:9). He also said in his model prayer "For thine is the Kingdom" (Matthew 6:13). He gives the instruction and how to draw near and he gives the source of power behind it. I have come to the realization that harmony with God will bring peace. With the regeneration power of the gospel in my life, I have experienced peace with God. I am able to be an ambassador of God's message of peace to a troubled world because I daily experience the peace of God in my life. My ministry is to be a channel of God's mercy, purity and peace.

There have been many times that I have stood between enemies. The Holy Spirit apparently was present to protect me. My attitude of peace caused such a stir and confusion that those enemies didn't know what to do. They would lay down their fists and with humility say "what should we do?" That gave me the opportunity to share the true peacemaker.

Drawing near to God involves an attitude of victory during persecution because it will bring about the Kingdom of heaven. "Blessed are they which are persecuted for righteousness sake" (Matthew 5:10). He also said in his model prayer "For thine is the power and the glory forever" (Matthew 6:13). He gives the instruction and how to draw near and he gives the source of power behind it. I have come to the realization that if persecuted, I am assured of the Kingdom of heaven. The Bible says, "Yea and all that will live godly in Christ Jesus shall suffer persecution" (2 Timothy 3:12). I know that suffering can be experienced through being kept from ones goal. I know that suffering can be experienced through being tempted through social enterprise. I know suffering can be felt through the presence of the world. I know suffering can be produced by fellow Christians. Some day I may experience suffering through physical abuse.

I can experience his power, presence and peace (Psalm 16:8). The key to spiritual victory is to stay close to God. I have to learn to practice God's presence all day long. "The Lord is near to all who call on him" (Psalm 145:18). The songwriter has written "Have thine own way Lord." During persecution and peace, I am going to celebrate life in magnifying Jesus' name.

Jesus never promised ease to those of us he called to follow him. Reliance upon Jesus will cause radical living. Ridicule will most likely pursue us but keep in mind a reward will follow. Jesus lived through persecution, he died through persecution and he rose again after the persecution.

Drawing near to God will fulfill God's promise that he will draw near to me. When I apply Jesus' instruction and experience his power through his model prayer, the Holy Spirit will produce his fruit in my life. The word "blessed" (Matthew 5:1-12) truthfully becomes a description of my life.

I have come to the end of this study and yet I have to return to the beginning with the word "blessed." Blessed means happy. My inner being is happy because of the work of God in my life. The characteristics I have been sharing have been a result of believing.

- I am learning to be helpless (poor in spirit).
- I am learning to be repentive (mournful).
- I am learning to be surrendered (meek).
- I am learning to crave (hunger).
- I am learning to practice empathy (mercy).

- I am learning to be authentic (pure).
- I am learning to be in harmony (peacemaker).
- I am learning to be victorious in suffering (persecution).

I am blessed with the Holy Spirit's enablement to experience a "touch of heaven" here on earth through practicing these attributes. I am realizing God's rule and providence in my life on earth. I am looking forward to when the last enemy (sin and death) (I Corinthians 15:24-28) will be destroyed at the Lord's return.

I am drawing near to him every day as I practice the Lord's instructions. The day will come when he will draw near to me even with greater intensity. "Face to face, I will behold him, far beyond the starry sky, Face to face, in all his glory, I shall see him by and by!" The only condition is faith in God's Son, the Lord Jesus Christ. He said, "For God so loved the world that he gave his only begotten son, that whoever believes on him should not perish but have everlasting life" (John 3:16).

I love my home here on earth. A day does not go by that as I walk in the yard with my dogs that I don't forget to thank God for the beauty and pleasantness of the place he has given me to live. I realize that my happiness is wherever my family is, that's home. As I draw near to God and he draws near to me, I can call heaven my eternal home. Death does not end all. My spirit lives on and enters immediately into the very presence of God.

Death involves physical and spiritual separation. Physical death occurs when my spirit is separated from the body. Spiritual death is the eternal separation of the spirit from God. This means that as a believer, I will never be separated from God. Jesus said "He who hears my word and believes in him who sent me has everlasting life" (John 5:24). In the deepest sense of the word, I will never die. Jesus gave the promise, "whoever lives and believes in me shall never die" (John 11:25, 26). Jesus is my source of life. He is the resurrection and the life. My life between death and resurrection will be a time of joy, blessing and fellowship with Jesus. Drawing near to him starts a deep and sweet relationship that will continue into a greater depth in heaven.

I am learning to live my life with a double citizenship. I am glad that I am a citizen of the United States of America and also of the heavenly city. A day is coming when our present solar system will be burned with fire and will be replaced by a new heaven and a new earth (2 Peter 3:10). It will burst into flames with such intense heat that even the elements that make up matter will be dissolved. The sun, the moon, the planets and the distant stars will all be engulfed in flames but this will not be a tragedy. The Bible says that out of the ruins will emerge a glorious new world — my eternal home (Revelation 21:1,2).

As I draw near to God and he draws near to me, he will bring me into a wonderful life. In my eternal home which is a perfect society, I will realize my full spiritual potential as an individual. I will enter in an eternal fellowship with God. An endless variety of meaningful activities will take place. All imperfections of this life will be gone and positive blessings will be in abundance. My present knowledge of God, while real and precious, is incomplete. In heaven I will know him perfectly. I will behold the glory of his presence and faith will turn to sight (Revelation 21:3).

If my attitude is based upon submission and obedience, God will draw near to me. He says, "I will draw near to you." This gives me a sense of his presence and love. To understand God's love, I have to know God's eternal passion to accomplish his will in such a way that he is glorified. God's love is eternal. God was love before he created man or anything else. I have to learn to let God be God. His will and glory go hand in hand to produce his love. I am under his umbrella of love. He unfolds his will to achieve his glory in my life through love.

The ultimate definition of God's love is expressed in these words: action, sacrifice, beneficial, unconditional and emotional. I must learn to take every circumstance of life and glorify him. The challenge is to be consumed with his love. I must keep his purpose in mind and then inner strength will flow.

He says, "I will draw near to you." This gives me a sense of his presence and grace. I do not deserve grace but God has given it to me. It is his unmerited favor. Grace is designed to save me and keep me. The Scripture says, "Grow in the grace and knowledge of our Lord and Savior Jesus Christ." (2 Peter 3:18). God is sufficient. God's grace is his empowerment to overcome. It raises me above the problem and gives me power at the exact point when I want to quit. Grace instructs me in how to live. Grace gives victory where I didn't have it. Grace will give the ability to keep going. Grace is the exchanging of my life for Christ-like living in me. (Galatians 2:20). Grace is inner spiritual power and not outward religious conformity. I have been set free to enjoy Christ's life in me (Galatians 5:1). I am challenged to measure my growth in grace; if I am lacking, I ask for his grace (Galatians 5:22,23).

He says, "I will draw near to you." This gives me a sense of his presence and sovereignty. He has absolute rule and control over all of creation. This means he causes or allows everything. I have to put everything in life under that perspective. It certainly makes me think, act and live different. He has created everything and he owns everything. He can do as he pleases. (Psalm 115:3; 135:6). Everything that occurs does so under the hand of a sovereign God. No chance happenings, no luck, no mistakes. Good and bad fall under his control. God knows where he is going and allows me to make choices. He will achieve his intended purpose. His purpose is to receive glory. I exist to please him (I Corinthians 8:6). I obtain strength through him (Philippians 4:13). I have confidence in him (2 Timothy 1:12).

He says, "I will draw near to you." This gives me a sense of his presence and glory. God's inner core is a radiating light (I Timothy 6:15,16). God's visible glory was most fully seen in the person of Jesus Christ (John 1:1,14,18). Jesus Christ is God in the flesh (Matthew 17:1-8). I am to tell of his glory (Psalm 96:1-3). His glory will put a glow in my life. Transformation is a growing adventure. I have to learn to submit to God's glory (I Corinthians 10:31). I glorify him when I

- Show Christ like character (John 15:8)
- Apply Biblical truths (Matthew 5:16)
- Practice sexual purity (I Corinthians 6:18-20)
- Daily confess sins (Joshua 7:19)
- Live by faith (Romans 4:19-21)
- Proclaim his Word (2 Thessalonians 3:1)
- Do his will (John 17:41)
- Confess his Son (Philippians 2:10)

He says, "I will draw near to you." This gives me a sense of his presence and justice. God is good, kind, loving and forgiving. He is also just and I must take his wrath seriously. God must judge sin because of the justice of his law and the righteousness of his character. He takes no pleasure in punishing the unrighteous (Ezekiel 33:11). He will judge all men according to their deeds (I Peter 1:17). The word "wrath" indicates God's intense displeasure of sin. God's wrath is not cruel but just. There are two sides to God's response to sin. "Thou hast loved righteousness and hated wickedness" (Psalm 45:7). I am glad that God is patient (2 Peter 3:9). My only way of escape is through God's substitute, Jesus who "delivers me from the wrath to come" (I Thessalonians 1:10). Christ died for me (Romans 5:8,9).

He says, "I will draw near to you." This gives me a sense of his presence and wisdom. Wisdom is knowing that God's purpose is to glorify himself. Wisdom moves all events, all people and all circumstances toward his purpose. Whether I resist or cooperate, he is still going to achieve his purpose. Wisdom is the ability to use my spiritual character, Biblical knowledge, common sense and circumstances and blending them together. I have an infinitely wise God that tells me to ask him for wisdom. I am not where I am by luck or chance. The infinitely wise God has been ordering my life. I was in his mind before the creation of the earth. He will give wisdom to make the response that will bring him glory. A determined will to agree with "thy will be done" is the answer. Ask in faith and anticipate the answer. Mixing human wisdom and divine wisdom doesn't work (James 3:16-18). To obtain wisdom, I have to admit that I need it. I have to stand in awe of God (Psalm 111:10). I have to study the Word. I need to pray for wisdom (James 1:5).

I will draw near to God. I have accepted the challenge and have followed his instruction through his "blessed sayings" and his model prayer with intensity. The fruit has become the test results. This has been evident in my life with his presence of love, grace, sovereignty, glory, justice and wisdom. He will keep to his Word. Experience it yourself! Why not try it! God's presence involves applying his instruction.

Teen Perspective

James 4:8 states "Draw near to me and I will draw near to you." See how it doesn't just simply say God will draw near to us. God calls us to himself, which means we need to put in effort to draw closer to our Lord. We aren' perfect, we are far from it, we can't do everything right, but it doesn't mean we can't try. God can and will help us each step of the way. As one reads through the Beatitudes in Matthew 5, it is almost like a guide, showing what will happen to those who are less fortunate. We can't just go to Jesus though, and ask Him to make everything right without actually repenting of our sins. The model or Lord's prayer can be another guide for us. After reading and applying all you've read in the Beatitudes as well as the Model Prayer, God will draw near unto you. Once we die, we will be as close to God as ever before. At that time, we will really be able to feel the 3 P's: His power, His presence, and His peace. Instead of feeling sorry for ourselves, we should flip all the bad things around, and use the situation to God's glory.

CHAPTER 13

What is the application results in glorifying God?

During my personal trial, I learned that God is enough, God's love is real, God's counsel is enduring, and God reigns supremely. I learned to interpret life from God's viewpoint. I learned to saturate my life with His thoughts. I learned to mix God's Word with faith. His word penetrated my mind, will and emotion. Faith is the ability to choose to fellowship with God, to obey Him, to love Him and to acknowledge him in all areas of life through complete submission and aggressive trust. I believe I am indwelt by the Spirit of God (Psalm 16:11). I have a constant active relationship with Jesus.

Going beyond myself and experiencing the supernatural started early in my life. Psalm 23:1 says, "The Lord is my shepherd". He is real to me. The shepherd became my savior and guide. I learned in my childhood to interpret life from God's point of view. I wanted to glorify God and it was demonstrated in following life's guidelines. Colossians 3:16 says, "Admonish in spiritual song". This would be a foundational step to follow. Each growth pattern would bring glory to God. Private tutoring would bring me to be approved by Board of Directors to the extension faculty at Sherwood Music School in Chicago. Director of bands started at Westside Christian Schools and ended at Plymouth Christian High School. They resulted in establishing fifty school curriculums and several Teacher of the Year Awards. Western Michigan University summer Music Camp appointed me as instrumental music counselor. I was presented the Distringuished Service Award from the Michigan Association of School Boards. I was selected teacher membership in music Teachers National Association and received a Doctor of sacred music degree from Maranatha Bible Seminary in Florida for Distinguished Attainment. The blessings brought glory to God.

Confirming God's love through the evidence of historical facts became my second motivation. Psalm 16:8 says, "I have set the Lord always before me". This has been my favorite verse since my teens. God would be my power, presence and peace throughout my life. I learned to saturate my life with His thoughts. I have been blessed by Gods words. The Bible has become my authority. The witness of divinity and my own spirit were united and I was truly blessed. After my childhood family gospel team and my teenage gospel team, I traveled across Michigan as itinerate pastor. This was turned into an interim ministry that brought more blessing and learning.

After a few short stays, I became Senior Pastor at Eastport Baptist Church. This church became my graduate study project and I was awarded a Doctorate in religion with a specialty in Biblical Christianity. Later, I became the first Associate Pastor at Mars Hill Bible Church and Visitation Pastor at Calvary Church. Glory to God was accomplished through growing, maturing in the faith and further ministry.

A Pastoral Health Care Ministry working with struggling in making spiritual, psychological and physiology adjustments followed.

Applying God's spiritual solutions to meet difficult trials have taught me to mix God's word with faith. My birth was a miracle. My parents didn't expect triplets. We were the only set of triplets born in our birth year. We are one of the oldest set recorded in the official records in our county. The God of the impossible is always present with His miraculous works. My life has been packed with adventurous faith. I have learned to draw near to God. This lead into organizational, administrative and mentorship during my 50 year ministry. Several of my books carry the witness of people worked with. With humility and thankful heart, I received a Certificate of Merit from the Northern Michigan Conciliation Service as their Board Chairman. The Northwest Antrim County Ministerial Association appointed me as their President. The Michigan State Senate Resolution No. 300 was given to the Kalamazoo Gospel Mission recognizing the Discipleship program of which I was director. The Louisiana Baptist University honored me with a Doctor of Ministry degree for integrating Christianity into the organizational development of several pastoral, educational and counseling ministries. My desire has been, "Be strong in the faith, giving glory to God" (Romans 4:20-21).

My most important blessing and glory is found in my family honoring God. They glorify God as a priority in life. I am thankful for their witness. I appreciate their dedication to God's word. I am encouraged with their faith.

My wife Joy, son John and daughter Amy and their families characterize with a mind which Christ thinks, a heart through which he loves and a voice through which Christ speaks, and a hand that which helps. Remember these verses, "We love because He first loved us" (I John 4:19, "Do all for the glory of God", I Corinthians 10:31, "Be of good courage and He shall strengthen your heart, all ye that hope in the Lord", Psalm 31:24.

Glorifying God will bring strength, support and steadfastness. It will show His greatness, graciousness, and goodness. His blessings will produce glory. I was in His mind before the creation of the earth. His presence of love, grace, sovereignty, glory, justice and wisdom has been in my journey.

Teen Perspective

Before I was even asked to write for this book, 1 Corinthians 10:31 was my favorite Bible verse, and a verse I tried to live by. When going through this book, my words just flowed onto the page. I now know more about this verse than I thought was possible. Even in my short sixteen years of life, God has shown His power to me in so many different ways, and He has been a huge part of my life. I had somewhat of a different first couple years of my life. I had heart problems when I was born and was able to have surgery at a young age, and everything went well. I was born in Russia and later adopted by people who I now know as my mom and dad. Through all that, I was never alone because God was always with me and watching over me. I've been through the pain of losing loved ones, including a young cousin and three grandparents, yet God held onto me and I to Him. God has led me each step of the way. He has given me happiness, success, and a wonderful life. I'm so thankful for everything He's done for me, and will continue to do for me.

Acknowledgements

I appreciate all the people that God has used to influence me. Many of these thoughts have come to my memory over the past seventy-nine years through sermon notes, lectures, conversations, meditations and reading. I have not knowingly withheld any significant reference from others in my devotional. To the best of my knowledge, all statements and information are true and correct and given credit. Everyone I have come in contact with should be given credit. Pastoral Health Care and Divine Dialogue Series is a constant source of encouragement.

About the Author

John F. Gillette's story begins and ends with a song he sang in his childhood, "His Very Own, Wonderful Grace in His Word is made known, chosen by the Father, purchased by the Son, sealed by the Spirit, I am his very own." His desire every day is to glorify the Lord Jesus Christ in health and in sickness. He has learned every moment needs to be in God's presence.

Divine dialogue is a developmental process. He has been a lifelong student of the Scriptures. It is easy to fail the standards of God but he has an inner passion that he calls "the holy urge" to encourage him to go forward. His studies have been in the liberal arts but always guided through his biblical deep rooted foundation. His graduate research has been in religion and leadership.

He has served Jesus Christ since his childhood with diversity, independence and confidence in education, pastorate and leadership. His pastoral health care discovery series was published to help himself and minister to others that are having struggles in making spiritual, psychological and physiological adjustments.

More Books in the Series:

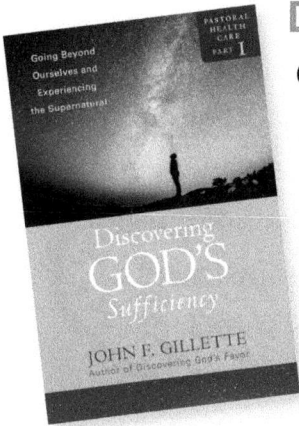

Discovering God's Sufficiency
Going Beyond Ourselves and Experiencing the Supernatural
Pastoral Health Care—Part One

Can anyone fix our troubles? The answer is 'yes.' How do we conquer our trials? We have to affirm God's intervention. We have to accept God's indwelling. We have to make some adjustments through God's illumination. We can experience God's power, presence and peace.

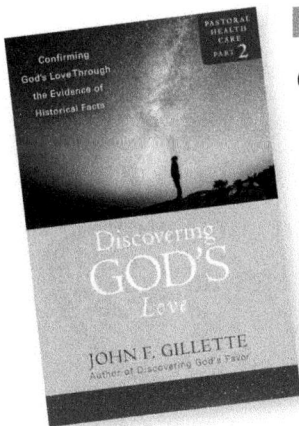

Discovering God's Love
Confirming God's love through the evidence of historical facts
Pastoral Health Care—Part Two

We can obtain strength to conquer through a knowledge of the 'Gospels' and receiving Jesus Christ into our hearts. The New Testament books of history give evidence of God's love. Through his love and faith, we are able to be strengthened, experience his support and become steadfast.

Available at www.schulerbooks.com/chapbook-press

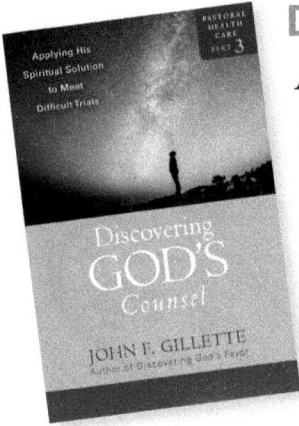

Discovering God's Counsel

Applying his spiritual solution to meet difficult trials

Pastoral Health Care—Part Three

Dark days can be life threatening. We have to develop an adequate level of spiritual, psychological and physiological adjustments. We can live with confidence in God's sufficiency.

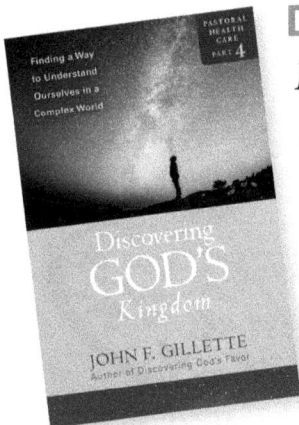

Discovering God's Kingdom

Finding a way to understand ourselves in a complex world

Pastoral Health Care—Part Four

Dealing with life, death, heaven and eternity with God's perspective is necessary. It involves a personal decision of belief, trust and faith. Knowledge and commitment will bring comfort and security. The eternal destiny directive will provide the way.

Available at www.schulerbooks.com/chapbook-press

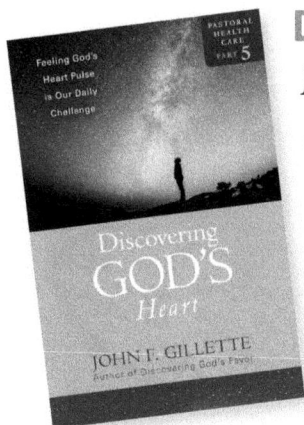

Discovering God's Heart

Feeling God's heart pulse is our daily challenge

Pastoral Health Care—Part Five

We have to practice the principles in the pastoral health care meditation method. We can handle any situation through thinking biblically. The spirit, soul and body are involved. Therefore, a holistic approach has to take place.

www.ingramcontent.com/pod-product-compliance
Ingram Content Group UK Ltd.
Pitfield, Milton Keynes, MK11 3LW, UK
UKHW020743150425
5479UKWH00045B/979